ACCA

Financial Management (FM)

Pocket Notes

British library cataloguing-in-publication data

A catalogue record for this book is available from the British Library.

Published by:
Kaplan Publishing UK
Unit 2 The Business Centre
Molly Millars Lane
Wokingham
Berkshire
RG41 2QZ

ISBN 978-1-78740-911-8

© Kaplan Financial Limited, 2021

Printed and bound in Great Britain.

Contents

The aim of the exam

The exam aims to develop the knowledge and skills at a managerial level in relation to financing, investment and dividend policy decisions.

The exam

- The syllabus is assessed by a three hour computer-based examination (CBE). Candidates are given an extra 10 minutes prior to the exam to read the exam instructions.
- All questions are compulsory.
- Section A of the exam comprises 15 multiple choice questions of 2 marks each.
- Section B of the exam comprises 15 scenario-based objective test case questions of 2 marks each (3 scenarios with 5 questions on each).
- Section C of the exam comprises two 20 mark questions.

The two 20 mark questions will mainly come from the working capital management, investment appraisal and business finance areas of the syllabus. The section A and section B questions can cover any areas of the syllabus. The balance between calculative and discursive elements of the questions is likely to be roughly 50/50.

Remember: much of accounting and finance is about explaining your figures – not simply calculating them. Don't forget to learn the assumptions of models (e.g. CAPM) and their strengths and weaknesses – easy marks can be gained this way.

If you are not already doing so – keep a file of past articles from the ACCA Student Accountant Magazine relevant to each paper you are studying. Those written about 6 to 12 months prior to exam often highlight likely exam topics (especially if they are written by the examining team).

Quality and accuracy are of the utmost importance to us so if you spot an error in any of our products, please send an email to mykaplanreporting@kaplan.com with full details, or follow the link to the feedback form in MyKaplan.

Our Quality Co-ordinator will work with our technical team to verify the error and take action to ensure it is corrected in future editions.

The financial management function

In this chapter

- The financial management function.
- Corporate strategy and corporate and financial objectives.
- Company objectives.
- Corporate stakeholders.
- Agency theory.
- Corporate governance.
- Measuring achievement of corporate objectives.
- Setting objectives in NFPs.
- Financial objectives.
- VFM.
- System analysis.

The financial management function

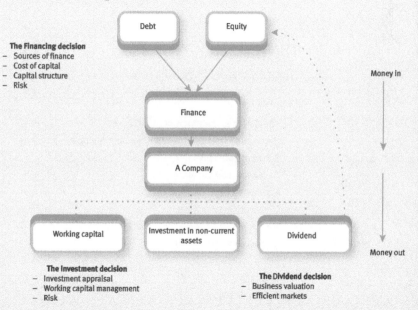

All decisions need to:

- control resources to ensure efficient and effective use

- consider the economic environment of the organisation

- consider risks and potential risks.

Key Point

Management accounting and financial management are concerned with resource usage to meet targets – however management accounting deals in short-term timescales and financial management is concerned with the longer-term.

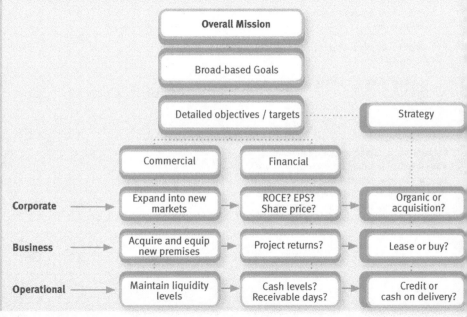

Corporate strategy and corporate and financial objectives

Overall Mission

Broad-based Goals

Detailed objectives / targets .... Strategy

	Commercial	Financial	
Corporate	Expand into new markets	ROCE? EPS? Share price?	Organic or acquisition?
Business	Acquire and equip new premises	Project returns?	Lease or buy?
Operational	Maintain liquidity levels	Cash levels? Receivable days?	Credit or cash on delivery?

Company objectives

The assumed primary aim of companies is shareholder wealth maximisation.

This objective underpins many of the techniques used in financial management e.g. the use of NPV for investment appraisal.

Other objectives could be:
- service levels
- quality
- staff welfare
- environmental concerns
- social responsibility
- profit maximisation
- growth
- market share.

Profit maximisation can be adopted as an objective, especially when managerial performance targets and rewards are linked to profit measures (e.g. ROCE). Potential problems with taking this approach are:

- short-termism
- risk
- non-cash based measures can permit manipulation of results.

The same concerns can also be applied to earnings per share growth.

Key Point

A distinction needs to be made between maximising (seeking the best possible outcome) and satisficing (finding a merely adequate outcome).

Remember the difference between profit and wealth generation!

Corporate stakeholders

Definition

A stakeholder group is one with a vested interest in the company.

Key Point

A stakeholder group is one with a vested interest in the company.

The company will thus have multiple objectives, often in conflict, and must seek to satisfy these through prioritisation and compromise.

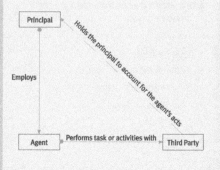

Agency theory

Objectives of shareholders (principals) and managers (agents) may not coincide – problem of **goal congruence**. Hence design of alternative remuneration schemes.

Examples

- A bonus based upon a minimum level of pre-tax profit.
- A bonus linked to the economic value added (EVA).
- A bonus based on turnover growth.
- An executive share option scheme (ESOP).

Examples of non-goal congruent behaviour undertaken by management

- Excessive remuneration levels.
- Empire building.
- Creative accounting.
- Off-balance-sheet financing.
- Inappropriate reaction to takeover bids.
- Unethical activities.

Managerial reward schemes should

- be clearly defined
- be easily monitored
- be impossible to manipulate
- link rewards to shareholder wealth
- encourage similar risk attitudes and time scales.

Corporate governance

Non-executive directors

- Important presence on the board.
- Must give obligation to spend sufficient time with the company.
- Should be independent.

Executive directors

- Separation of chairman and CEO.
- Submit for re-election.
- Clear disclosure of emoluments.
- At least matched in number by NEDs.

Key Point

Adherence to the Combined Code of Corporate Governance is voluntary, but a listed company is expected to comply and if it does not it must explain why.

Measuring achievement of corporate objectives

Key Point

Ratio analysis compares and quantifies relationships between financial variables.

More details of financial ratios are in Chapter 19.

Setting objectives in NFPs

The primary objective of not-for-profit organisations is not to make profit but to benefit prescribed groups of people.

Key issues when planning within NFPs are as follows.

- Multiple objectives, which are often harder to prioritise – e.g. in a hospital, treating more patients v better patient care.

- While costs may be easy to measure, the benefits and performance are often notoriously difficult to quantify – e.g. quality of patient care.

- The influence of funding bodies – e.g. the Government – and their objectives.

- It may be difficult to measure objectives as they are often non-financial (e.g. reducing suffering caused by a natural disaster).

- Wide range of stakeholders with a high level of interest.

- Long-term planning horizons.

- Funding may be a series of advances and not a lump sum.

- Little or no financial input from the ultimate recipients of the service.

In NFPs the non-financial objectives are often more important and more complex.

Financial objectives

Services provided are limited by the funds available.

Key objectives for not-for-profit organisations:
- raise as large a sum as possible
- spend funds as effectively as possible.

Targets are set per period.
- Total to be raised in grants and voluntary income.
- Maximum percentage of this total that fund-raising expenses represents.
- Amounts to be spent on specified projects or in particular areas.

- Maximum permitted administration costs.
- Meeting budgets.
- Breaking-even in the long run.
- Other measures: waiting time, successful outcomes etc.

Actuals compared to targets.

Control action taken if necessary.

VFM

'Value for money' is 'achieving the desired level and quality of service at the most economical cost'.

- VFM is important due to the nature of NFPs and because they are facing an increasing need for accountability.

- It is generally taken to mean the pursuit of economy, efficiency and effectiveness.

- **Effectiveness** is a measure of outputs, i.e. services/facilities – e.g. number of pupils taught, % achieving key stage targets. Effectiveness can only be measured with respect to the organisation's objectives.

- **Efficiency** is the measure of outputs over inputs, i.e. resource utilisation – e.g. average class size, cost per pupil.

- **Economy** is being effective and efficient at the lowest possible cost. For example, by adopting commercial purchasing techniques.

System analysis

Systems analysis and performance measurement can be used in assessing VFM.

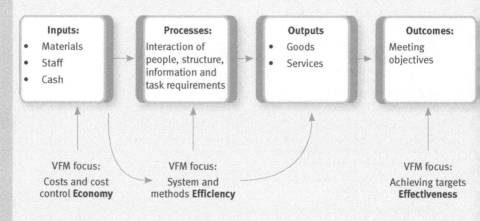

This chapter tends to be examined as part of a larger question.

You must be able to confidently discuss the key functions of a financial manager.

Recent FM (previously known as F9) exams containing these topics include:

- December 2011 – Bar Co
- June 2013 – HDW Co
- Dec 2013 – Darn Co
- June 2014 – MFZ Co
- Mar/Jun 2019 – Pinks Co

2

Basic investment appraisal techniques

In this chapter

- Accounting profits and cashflows.
- ROCE (Accounting Rate of Return – ARR).
- Payback.

Accounting profits and cash flows

(a) Cash flows are better than profits

   (i) Cash can be spent – profits are only a guide to the cash that may be available.

   (ii) Profit measurement is subjective, cash is real.

   (iii) Cash can be used to pay dividends.

(b) Use relevant cash flows – future, incremental cash flows and opportunity costs

   (i) Future

     Ignore sunk costs

   (ii) Incremental

     Ignore committed costs

     Ignore apportioned costs

   (iii) Cash flows

     Ignore depreciation

   (iv) Opportunity costs

     Include value of cash flow of best missed opportunity

(c) Ignore interest payments on funding to avoid double counting with cost of capital

(d) Include tax payments and receipts

ROCE (Accounting Rate of Return – ARR)

Definition

$$ROCE = \frac{\text{Average annual profit before interest and tax}}{\text{Initial capital costs}} \times 100\%$$

Alternatively you may be asked to use the average capital instead of the initial capital. Average capital is calculated as:

(Initial capital + scrap value) / 2

Key Point

- Errors are often made through trying to calculate ROCE using relevant cash flows – it is a profit based measure, not a cash flow-based measure.

- Similarly, the project investment should include book values of assets employed.

Strengths

- Expressed in terms familiar to managers – profit and capital employed.

- Easy to calculate the likely effect of the project on the reported profit and loss account/balance sheet. Managers are frequently rewarded in relation to performance against these variables.

- Businesses are judged on return on investment measures by financial markets.

Limitations

- Does not ensure that shareholder wealth is maximised.

- Figures easily manipulated.

- Ignores the actual/incremental cash flows associated with the project.

Payback

Definition

The time taken to recoup the initial cash outlay on a project.

$$\text{Payback period} = \frac{\text{Initial payment}}{\text{Annual cash flow}}$$

If cash flows are uneven then payback is calculated using the **cumulative cash flow** over the life of the investment.

Payback might not be an exact number of years.

Organisations set target payback periods and will probably reject projects which have paybacks longer than the target.

Strengths

- Simple to calculate and understand
- It favours quick return
  - helps company grow
  - minimises risk
  - maximises liquidity.

Limitations

- Does not ensure that shareholder wealth is maximised.
- Ignores timing of cash flows.
- Ignores returns after the payback period.
- It is subjective – no definitive investment decision.

Exam focus

Recent FM (previously known as F9) exams
containing these topics include

- September 2016 – Fence Co
  (Qs 26 – 30)

3

Investment appraisal: discounted cash flow techniques

In this chapter

- The time value of money.
- Compounding.
- Discounting.
- Net present value.
- Internal rate of return (IRR).
- NPV v IRR.

The time value of money

Definition

Money received today is worth more than the same sum received in the future because of:

- the potential for earning interest
- the impact of inflation
- the effect of risk.

Key Point

DCF techniques take account of the time value of money when appraising investments.

Compounding

Definition

The terminal value is the value in n years' time, of a sum invested now, at an interest rate of r%.

Compounding calculates the future or terminal value of a given sum of money.

$$F = P(1 + r)^n$$

where F = Future value after n periods

P = Present or Initial value

r = Rate of interest per period

n = Number of periods

KAPLAN PUBLISHING

Discounting

Definition

Discounting is the conversion of future cash flows to their value at one point in time – usually the present day.

The **present value** is the cash equivalent now of money receivable/payable at some future date.

The present value (P) of a future sum (F) receivable or payable at time n, using a discount rate r%, can be calculated using the formula:

$$P = \frac{F}{(1+r)^n} = F \times (1+r)^n$$

$(1 + r)^{-n}$ is called the **discount factor**.

An **annuity** is a constant annual cash flow for a number of years. The present value (P) can be found using an annuity formula or annuity tables.

The present value of an annuity is found using the formula

$$P = \frac{annual}{cashflow} \times \frac{1 - (1+r)^n}{r}$$

$\dfrac{1 - (1+r)^n}{r}$ is known as the **annuity factor**.

A **perpetuity** is an annual cash flow that occurs for ever – in exams it may be described as 'for the foreseeable future'.

The present value (P) of a perpetuity is found using the formula:

$$P = \frac{Annual\ cash\ flow}{Interest\ rate} \quad or$$

$$P = \frac{Annual}{cash\ flow} \times \frac{1}{r}$$

$\dfrac{1}{r}$ is known as the **perpetuity factor**.

Some regular cash flows may start later than T_1. These are dealt with by applying the appropriate factor to the cash flow as normal and then discounting your answer back to T_0.

e.g. annuity factor for a five year annuity starting at time period 3 = annuity factor$^{1-5}$ × 2 year discount factor

For regular cash flows that start at time period 0, ignore the first cash flow and add 1 to the factor for the remaining cash flows.

e.g. For a 7 year annuity starting at t0, annuity factor = (1 + 6 year annuity factor)

Exam focus

Unless told otherwise assume:

- all cash flows occur at the start or end of a year.

- initial investments occur at once (T_0).

- other cash flows start in one year's time (T_1).

Discount Tables

Use the present value tables to calculate the present value of one cash flow in the future.

Use the annuity tables to calculate the present value of a series of equal annual cash flows.

Present value and annuity tables are provided in the exam.

When discounting, the rate the company should apply to take account of the time value of money may be referred to as:

- cost of capital

- rate of return

- discount rate

- required return

- weighted average cost of capital.

Net Present Value

All future cash flows are discounted to the present value and then added.

Present value = future value x discount factor.

The NPV represents the surplus funds (after funding the investment) earned on the project, therefore:

- if the NPV is positive – the project is financially viable
- if the NPV is zero – the project breaks even
- if the NPV is negative – the project is not financially viable.

Advantages

- It considers the time value of money.
- It is an absolute measure of return.
- It is based on cash flows not profits.
- It considers the whole life the project.
- It should lead to the maximisation of shareholders' wealth.
- Higher discount rates can be set for riskier projects.

Limitations

- Not easily explained to managers.
- Requires that the cost of capital is known.

Internal rate of return (IRR)

The rate of interest (discount) at which the NPV = 0.

May be found by linear interpolation or extrapolation.

The formula for the IRR is:

$$IRR \approx L + \left[\frac{N_L}{N_L - N_H} \times (H - L) \right]$$

Where L = Lower rate of interest

H = Higher rate of interest

N_L = NPV at lower rate of interest

N_H = NPV at higher rate of interest

Projects should be accepted if their IRR is greater than the cost of capital.

Exam focus

This formula is not provided in the exam. You must learn it.

Advantages

- Does consider the time value of money.
- A percentage is easily understood.
- Uses cash flows.
- It considers the whole life of the project.
- It does not need the cost of capital to be known.

Limitations

- It is not a measure of absolute profitability.
- It is fairly complicated to calculate.
- Interpolation only provides an estimate.
- Non-conventional cash flows may give rise to multiple IRRs.

NPV v IRR

- Both superior to basic techniques.
- The two methods can give conflicting advice.

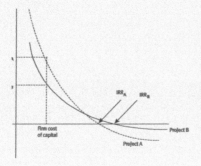

- Since NPV tells us the absolute increase in shareholder wealth it is the better technique for choosing between 2 mutually exclusive projects.

Exam focus

Investment appraisal is a core topic and is likely to be examined every sitting.

Recent FM (previously known as F9) exams containing basic discounted cash flow techniques include:

- December 2011 – Warden
- June 2013 – HDW Co
- December 2013 – Darn Co
- June 2014 – OAP Co
- December 2014 – Uftin Co
- June 2015 – Hraxin Co
- Sep / Dec 2015 – Argnil Co
- Mar/Jun 2016 – Degnis Co
- December 2016 – Dysxa Co
- Mar/Jun 2017 – Vyxyn Co
- Sep/Dec 2018 – Melanie Co

Investment appraisal: further aspects of discounted cash flow

In this chapter

- Inflation.
- Taxation.
- Working capital.

Inflation

Inflation features in approximately half of all exam NPV questions. The main error students make is to confuse the two main approaches for dealing with inflation.

Definition

Inflation is a general increase in prices leading to a general decline in the real value of money.

Lenders require a return made up of the real return (that required if there was no inflation) and an additional return just to keep up with inflation.

Inflation affects both future cash flows and the discount rate used.

Cash flows

Current cash flows: cash flows may be expressed in today's terms ("current terms")

Money cash flows: cash flows may have future inflation incorporated ("money" or "nominal terms").

Real cash flows: cash flows expressed in "real" terms are money cash flows with the general rate of inflation stripped out

Exam focus

Make sure you know the difference between these terms. "Money" flows are flows of actual amounts of money, i.e. inflation is taken into account.

Discount rates

Discount rates may exclude inflation ("real rate") or incorporate future inflation ("money rates"):

r = real discount rate

i = money discount rate

h = inflation rate

$$(1+r) = \frac{(1+i)}{(1+h)}, \quad (1+i) = (1+r)(1+h)$$

Finding NPV with inflation – two methods

Real Method
Real cash flows : real rate

- Do not inflate the cash flows. Leave them expressed in current terms (today's prices).

- Discount at the real rate.

Useful if given uninflated cash flows and there is a single rate of inflation.

Nominal (Money) method
Money cash flows : money rate

- Inflate the cash flows to find the money values (using the inflation rate).

- Discount at the money rate.

Useful if different cash flows are subject to different rates of inflation – known as 'specific inflation'.

The two methods give the same NPV.

Exam focus

In an exam, for a short-life project with the cash flows inflating at different rates set out the NPV calculations with the cash flows down the side and time across the top. Show how you calculated each figure in workings set out below and cross-referenced to your NPV calculations.

Recently the examiner has asked for an NPV calculation using the real method when there is more than one inflation value in the question. The technique to use for this is to inflate the cash flows to money cash flows and then deflate them at the general inflation rate. Then discount them using the real cost of capital.

Taxation

DCF and taxation

There are two important tax effects to consider.

(a) Tax payments on operating profits.

(b) Tax benefit from tax-allowable depreciation and a possible tax payment from a balancing charge on asset disposal.

Tax relief on interest payments on debt is taken into account by adjusting the discount rate. See chapter 15.

Exam focus

Most exam questions on NPV involve taxation.

Basic idea

The presence of tax in a question essentially means that there are more cash flows to include. With the exception of working capital

cash flows, all relevant cash flows should have a tax consequence that also needs to be included.

- **Trading cash flows**
  Trading cash flows such as sales, wages, etc will be taxed at the tax rate given in the question. The simplest way of dealing with these is to calculate a net total and apply the tax rate to that figure.

- **Asset cash flows**
  Initial investment will attract tax relief through tax-allowable depreciation. Usually 25% reducing balance, with a balancing allowance or charge when the asset is sold or scrapped.

Exam focus

The tax-allowable depreciation calculation should be fairly routine and a source of easy marks in an exam.

Normal assumptions

(a) Tax may be delayed by a year, or there may be no delay. READ THE QUESTION.

(b) It is normally assumed that the company is generating sufficient taxable profits so as to be able to absorb all allowances in full at the earliest opportunity.

(c) Assume that the initial capital expenditure happens immediately at time period 0 and that the first tax-allowable depreciation will be available at time period 1.

Exam focus

Read the question carefully to ensure you pick up the correct timings.

Tax-allowable depreciation and tax savings calculations (e.g. 4 year investment) assuming tax payments are made one year after the accounting year end

Year	Description	CA calculation	Tax saved	Timing if 1 year delay
0	Investment	X		
1	Tax-allowable depreciation (25%)	(X)	x 30% =	Year 2
2	Book Value Tax-allowable (25%)	X (X)	x 30% =	Year 3
3	Book Value Tax-allowable (25%)	X (X)	x 30% =	Year 4
4	Book Value Balancing Allowance Residual value	X (X) X	x 30% =	Year 5

The examiner has stressed the area of investment appraisal for examining – remember when doing an investment appraisal to think about your layout – set your figures out in a table and list the workings underneath – cross-referencing them in the table. Use plenty of space – this makes the marker's job easier and means they won't miss key figures (and marks).

Pro Forma for the NPV calculation for the above four year project (assuming tax is delayed one year)

	t = 0	t = 1	t = 2	t = 3	t = 4	t = 5
Sales receipts		X	X	X	X	
Costs		(X)	(X)	(X)	(X)	
Operating cash flows		**X**	**X**	**X**	**X**	
Tax payable = Operating cash flows × tax rate			(X)	(X)	(X)	(X)
Investment	(X)					
Residual value					X	
Tax savings on Tax-allowable depreciation (separate working)			X	X	X	X
Working capital flows	(X)				X	
Net cash flows	(X)	X	X	X	X	X
Discount factors	1	x	x	x	x	x
Present Value	(X)	X	X	X	X	X

The five headings in bold must be prepared for all NPV questions involving taxation.

This layout is particularly useful when a question involves both tax and inflation.

Key Point

When answering questions which contain both tax and inflation remember to use the money method.

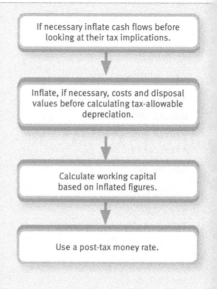

If necessary inflate cash flows before looking at their tax implications.

Inflate, if necessary, costs and disposal values before calculating tax-allowable depreciation.

Calculate working capital based on inflated figures.

Use a post-tax money rate.

Working capital

Simple questions

Working capital is treated as an investment at the start of the project. Any increases during the project are treated as a relevant cash outflow.

At the end of the project the working capital is 'released' – an inflow.

More complex questions

The working capital requirement is given as a % of (usually) sales.

Changes in the working capital requirement give rise to relevant cash flows. Any increase in the requirement is a cash outflow, any decrease an inflow.

Exam focus

Recent FM (previously known as F9) exams containing further aspects of discounted cash flow techniques include:

- June 2013 – HDW Co
- December 2013 – Darn Co
- June 2014 – OAP Co
- December 2014 – Uftin Co
- June 2015 – Hraxin Co
- Sep / Dec 2015 – Argnil Co
- Mar / Jun 2016 – Degnis Co
- September 2016 – Hebac Co
- December 2016 – Dysxa Co
- Mar / Jun 2017 – Vyxyn Co
- Sep / Dec 2017 – Pelta Co
- Mar / Jun 2019 – Pinks Co

chapter

5

Asset investment decisions and capital rationing

In this chapter

- Lease versus buy decision.
- Replacement decisions.
- Capital rationing.

Lease versus buy decision

Key Point

Lease or (borrow to) buy decision

The decision to purchase has already been made. The financing decision can now be made comparing the use of a lease to that of buying.

Discount rate to be used

The assumption is that buying requires the use of a bank loan (for the sake of comparability). The user will receive allowances against the interest payable on the loan; this affects the discount rate so use the Post-Tax Cost of Borrowing.

Post-tax cost of borrowing = Pre-tax cost of borrowing x (1-t).

Cash flows

Leasing

1 Rental payments (usually in advance).
2 Tax relief on the rental payments.

Buying

1 The purchase cost.
2 Any residual value.
3 Any associated tax implications due to tax-allowable depreciation on the asset.

Evaluation

Determine the present value cost of leasing and compare this to the present value cost of borrowing to buy.

Key Point

Be careful with the timings of your cash flows, especially under the leasing option.

Replacement decisions

This technique can be used when the assets of the project need replacing periodically, by new assets.

Key ideas/assumptions

1. Cash inflows from trading are not normally considered in this type of question.

2. The difficulty will arise from the differing lifecycles of each machine.

3. The operating efficiency of machines will be similar.

4. The assets will be replaced in perpetuity or at least into the foreseeable future.

Definition

The Equivalent Annual Cost (EAC) is the equal annual cash flow (annuity) to which a series of uneven cash flows is equivalent to in present value terms.

$$\text{Equivalent annual cost} = \frac{\text{PV of costs}}{\text{Annuity factor}}$$

To calculate the optimum replacement cycle you should:

(1) Calculate the NPV of each replacement cycle.

(2) Calculate the EAC for each cycle.

(3) Choose the cycle with the lowest EAC.

Capital rationing

Shareholder wealth is maximised if a company undertakes all possible positive NPV projects. Capital rationing is where there are insufficient funds to do so.

Hard Capital Rationing

An absolute limit on the amount of finance available imposed by the lending institutions. There are two considerations:

- industry wide factors limiting funds
- company specific factors.

Soft capital rationing

A company may impose its own rationing on capital e.g. from a desire to control the rate of expansion. This is contrary to the rational view which would hold that if a project yields a positive NPV then it is worth doing.

Methods for solving capital rationing problems

- **Divisible projects**

  Calculate the profitability index (NPV per $1 needed in the capital restricted period) and allocate the funds in order of their profitability indexes.

  $$\text{Profitability index} = \frac{\text{NPV}}{\text{Investment needed in capital} - \text{restricted period}}$$

- **Indivisible projects**

  Use trial and error to find the combination of projects with the highest total net present value.

- **Mutually exclusive projects**

  Choose the project with the highest NPV.

Exam focus

Recent FM (previously known as F9) exams containing asset investment decisions and capital rationing include:

- December 2011 – Warden
- June 2014 – OAP Co
- Sep / Dec 2015 – Argnil Co
- December 2016 – Dysxa Co
- Sep / Dec 2018 – Melanie Co
- Sep / Dec 2019 – Dink Co

chapter

6

Investment appraisal under uncertainty

In this chapter

- Risk.
- Uncertainty.

Investment appraisal faces the following problems

- All decisions are based on forecasts.
- All forecasts are subject to uncertainty.
- This uncertainty needs to be reflected in the financial evaluation.

Risk

It is essential to distinguish between risk which is quantifiable and uncertainty which is not.

Risk allows the use of mathematical models to aid in the decision making process as the probabilities of different outcomes can be estimated.

In investment appraisal the areas of concern are therefore the accuracy of estimates concerning:

- Project life
- Predicted cash flows and their probabilities
- Discount rate used.

Methods used to take risk into consideration in investment appraisal:

1 Probability analysis

Use a probability distribution of outcomes and calculate an expected value E(X).

$E(X) = \sum px$

Where p is the probability of each outcome and x is the cash flow from each outcome.

Advantages of EVs

- Quantifies probabilities
- Simple calculations
- Deals with multiple outcomes

Disadvantages of EVs

- answer is a long-run average
- probabilities are subjective
- ignores investors attitude to risk
- ignores the variabilities of payoffs.

The EV rule is appropriate if:

- there is a reasonable basis for making the forecasts and estimates
- the decision and risk are small in relation to the business
- the decision is a common one for the business i.e. repetitive.

The probability distribution can also be used to measure risk by:

- calculating the worst possible outcome and its probability
- calculating the probability that the project will fail
- assessing the standard deviation of the outcomes.

2 **Discounted Payback Period or Payback used in addition to NPV analysis**

Payback measures how long it takes for the initial cash outlay to be recouped. All other things being equal, the longer the payback period the higher the risk as cash flows far in the future are more difficult to predict and subject to more unexpected events.

3 **Risk – adjusted discount rates**

- If the project is significant in size and likely to result in additional risks, then a project specific or risk adjusted discount rate should be used.

- Increase the discount rates by adding a risk premium. or use the CAPM with a risk appropriate beta factor (see chapter 17) to calculate a revised cost of equity.

Uncertainty (probabilities of different outcomes cannot be estimated)

1 Sensitivity analysis

Calculate how much one input value must change before the decision changes (say from accept to reject).

This maximum possible change is often expressed as a percentage;

$$\text{Sensitivity margin} = \frac{\text{NPV}}{\text{PV of flow under consideration}} \times 100\%$$

The smaller the margin the more sensitive is the decision to the factor being considered.

For sensitivity to the discount rate, calculate the percentage change needed to the cost of capital to get to the IRR.

Sensitivity Analysis – advantages

- Allows managers to make better judgements by providing them with information as to the critical estimates.
- Simple to calculate and understand.

Sensitivity Analysis – disadvantages

- Does not assess the chance of a variable changing.
- Ignores interrelationships between variables.
- Does not provide a decision rule.

2 Set shorter payback targets

The longer the payback period the higher the risk as cash flows far in the future are more difficult to predict and subject to more unexpected events.

3 Using prudent estimates assess the worst possible situation

Concentrate on the down-side. Suits projects where investors are very risk averse or where project failure would be disastrous.

4 Obtain a range of NPVs by assessing the worst and best possible situations

Gives investors an idea about the range of possible project outcomes. Whether the project is acceptable or not will depend on investors' personal attitudes to risk.

5 Simulation

- Looks at the impact of many variables changing at the same time.

- Uses mathematical models to produce a distribution of the possible outcomes from the project and allows their probabilities to be calculated.

Advantages of simulation

- It includes all possible outcomes in the decision-making process.
- Easily understood technique.
- It has a wide variety of applications.
- Works in complex situations which are difficult to model mathematically in other ways.

Disadvantages of simulation

- Models can become extremely complex.
- Time and costs involved in their construction can be more than is gained from the improved decisions.
- Probability distributions may be difficult to formulate.

Recent FM (previously known as F9) exams containing questions on risk and uncertainty include:

- June 2010 – ZSE Co (expected values)
- June 2011 – BRT Co
- December 2011 – Warden
- June 2015 – Hraxin Co
- Mar / Jun 2016 – Degnis Co
- December 2016 – Dysxa Co
- Mar/Jun 2017 – Vyxyn Co
- Mar / Jun 2018 – Copper Co

Working capital management

In this chapter

- Working capital.
- Working capital management.
- Cash operating cycle.
- Working capital ratios.
- Interpreting working capital ratios.
- Liquidity.
- Working capital investment levels.

Working capital

Definition

Working capital is that capital available for conducting the day-to-day operations of the business – it is generally current assets minus current liabilities.

Key Point

All aspects of both current assets and current liabilities need to be managed to:

- minimise the risk of insolvency
- maximise the return on assets.

The optimum level of working capital is the amount that results in no idle resources without strain on liquid resources.

The management of working capital can also be seen as determining the trade-off between profitability and liquidity.

Investing in working capital has a cost (the cost of funding or opportunity cost of the funds being unavailable for other uses).

To increase funding an organisation can:

- decrease the level of current assets
- increase the level of current liabilities.

Working capital management

Key Point

Remember that current assets are often especially important in small companies.

Mismanagement of working capital can lead to business failure.

- Insolvency due to lack of liquid assets.
- Overtrading.
- Overstocking.
- Excessive investment in working capital.

Indicators of overtrading

- Rapid increase in turnover.
- Rapid increase in current assets.
- Increase in inventory and receivables collection period.
- Increased reliance on short-term finance, such as trade payables or overdrafts.
- Increase in trade payables days
- Decrease in current and quick ratio.

Cash operating cycle

(cash cycle or trading cycle)

The operating cycle is the length of time between the company's outlay on raw materials, wages and other expenditures and the inflow of cash from the sale of goods.

Cash operating cycle

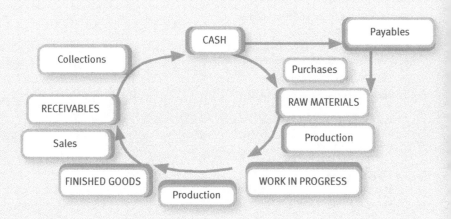

The length of the cycle = Inventory days + Receivable days – Payables days.

Measured in days, weeks or months.

Inventory days for manufacturing = raw materials holding period+ WIP holding period+ finished goods holding period.

The amount of cash required to fund the operating cycle will increase as either:

- the cycle gets longer
- the level of activity / Sales increases.

Reduce cycle in time by:

- improving production efficiency
- improving finished goods and/or raw material inventory turnover
- improving receivables collection and payables payment periods.

Influences on the cash operating cycle:

- industry influence
- growth
- inflation
- liquidity versus profitability decisions
- management efficiency.

Working capital ratios

Current ratio	$\dfrac{\text{Current assets}}{\text{Current liabilities}}$		
Quick ratio/Acid test	$\dfrac{\text{Current assets} - \text{Inventory}}{\text{Current liabilities}}$		
Receivables' collection period (in days)	$\dfrac{\text{Receivables}}{\text{Daily sales}}$	or	$\dfrac{\text{Receivables} \times 365}{\text{Total sales}}$
Payables' payment period (in days)	$\dfrac{\text{Payables}}{\text{Daily purchases}}$	or	$\dfrac{\text{Payables} \times 365}{\text{Total purchases}}$

Inventory holding period (days)	$\dfrac{\text{Inventory}}{\text{Cost of sales}} \times 365$
This can be split further in manufacturing companies as :	
(a) Raw materials	$\dfrac{\text{Stock of raw materials}}{\text{Raw materials usage*}} \times 365$ *Where usage cannot be calculated, purchases gives a good approximation
(b) Work in progress	$\dfrac{\text{Work in progress}}{\text{Cost of production}} \times 365$
(c) Finished goods	$\dfrac{\text{Stock of finished goods}}{\text{Cost of sales}} \times 365$
Inventory turnover	$\dfrac{\text{Total cost of sales}}{\text{Average inventory held}}$

- When comparing ratios between two balance sheets you can base each holding period on balance sheet figures rather than an average.

- Don't forget turnover figures (the inverse of the ratios discussed above).

- The multiples in the ratios is 365 for days, 52 for weeks and 12 for months.

Interpreting working capital ratios

In exam questions try to make your comments as relevant as possible to the scenario. In particular look for information on any of the following and tailor your comments accordingly.

- The industry within which the firm operates.

- The type of products sold.
- Whether products are manufactured or bought in.
- The level of sales.
- Inventory and credit policies.
- The cash operating cycle.
- The efficiency with which working capital is managed.

Ratios have limitations – the figures may not be representative, there may be seasonal fluctuations and there may be window dressing.

Ratios are concerned with the past and may be distorted by growth or inflation.

It is important to look at several ratios in conjunction to obtain an overall impression of the company.

As with all ratios, you ideally want a basis for comparison.

- Actual v budget.
- This year v last year.
- This firm v industry average.

Inventory

- In general the lower the ratio the better.
- Inventory is expensive to hold.

Receivables

- Generally the lower the ratio the better.

Payables

Increasing payables days increases credit, but:

- lose prompt payment discounts
- suppliers may increase prices to compensate
- may lose supplier goodwill.

Liquidity

- Current ratio and quick ratio measure liquidity.
- Usually the higher the ratio the more liquidity an organisation has.
- Benchmarks are often given as 2:1 for the current ratio and 1:1 for the quick ratio.

Working capital investment levels

Factors influencing working capital investment levels

- Nature of the company.
- Uncertainty as to deliveries from suppliers.
- Activity levels.
- Company's credit policy.
- Length of the operating cycle.
- Credit policy of suppliers.
- Risk appetite of company.

Working capital ratios can be used to predict working capital investment levels required in the future.

Exam focus

Recent FM (previously known as F9) exams containing general aspects on working capital management include:

- December 2013 – Plot Co
- June 2015 – Widnor Co
- Sep / Dec 2015 – ZXC Co
- Mar / Jun 2016 – Crago Co
- Mar / Jun 2017 – Pangli Co
- Sep / Dec 2018 – Oscar Co
- Mar / Jul 2020 – Pumice Co

Working capital management – inventory control

In this chapter

- Managing inventory.
- Economic order quantity.
- Inventory management systems.
- Just-in-time inventory management.

Managing inventory

> Need to maintain a balance between liquidity (low inventory levels) and profitability (sufficient inventory to meet customer needs).

Costs

Material costs are a major part of a company's costs and need to be carefully controlled.

There are four types of cost associated with inventory:

- ordering costs
- holding costs
- inventory out costs
- and the purchase cost.

However

Costs of low inventory levels:

- lost contribution due to **stockouts**
- production stoppages
- emergency orders
- high re-order costs
- high set-up costs
- lost quantity discounts.

Inventory management includes determining:

- optimum re-order level
- optimum re-order quantity
- a balance between holding costs and stock out and reorder costs (i.e. liquidity and profitability).

Lead time is the lag between when an order is placed and the item is delivered.

Buffer inventory is the basic level of inventory which is kept for emergencies.

Economic order quantity

The aim of the EOQ model is to minimise the total cost of holding and ordering inventory; the re-order point which does this is known as the Economic Order Quantity.

Formula

Annual Ordering Cost = $C_o \times \dfrac{D}{Q}$

Annual Holding Cost = $C_h \times \dfrac{Q}{2}$

Annual holding cost if buffer inventory present = $C_h \times (Q/2 + buffer)$

Where:

$$EOQ = \sqrt{\dfrac{2C_oD}{C_h}}$$

C_o = Cost per order
D = Annual demand
C_h = Cost of holding one unit for one year
Q = Quantity ordered

Assumptions

- Demand and lead time are known.
- Demand and lead time are constant.
- Purchase price is constant.
- No buffer inventory is held.

Key Point

If any of the above assumptions do not hold then the model may be invalid.

Total annual inventory costs = purchase costs + ordering costs + holding costs

= P*D + Co × D/Q + Ch × Q/2

Note: Where buffer inventory is held, holding costs become Ch × (Q/2 + buffer)

Quantity discounts

Step 1 Calculate EOQ, ignoring discounts.

Step 2 If this is below the level for discounts, calculate total annual inventory costs.

Step 3 Recalculate total annual inventory costs using the order size required to just obtain the discount.

Step 4 Compare the cost of steps 2 and 3 with the saving from the discount, and select the minimum cost alternative.

Step 5 Repeat for all discount levels.

Calculating the re-order level

- The re-order level (ROL) is the volume of inventory held when an order is placed.

- If demand and lead time are certain then ROL = demand in the lead time.

Inventory management systems

- Periodic review.
- JIT.

Periodic review systems

- Inventory levels reviewed at fixed intervals.

- Inventory is then made up to a predetermined level.

- The level is set based on demand and demand in the lead time.

- Popular with suppliers.

- Easier to plan administration and spreads work evenly.

Just-in-time inventory management

An alternative view of inventory management is the reduction or elimination of inventory, since inventory is seen as waste.

Key Point

Aims of JIT are:

- a smooth flow of work through the manufacturing plant
- a flexible production process which is responsive to the customer's requirements
- reduction in capital tied up in inventory.

To obtain this:

- batch sizes are reduced
- raw material inventory is delivered to point of use
- processes are designed to allow JIT and also quality to be maximised
- finished goods are made to order.

Suppliers need to:

- have high levels of quality and reliability
- build long-term trusting relationships
- be physically close.

Exam focus

Recent FM (previously known as F9) exams featuring questions on inventory control include:

- December 2010 – WQZ Co
- December 2013 – Plot Co
- September 2016 – Nesud Co
- Sep / Dec 2019 – Dusty Co

Working capital management – accounts payable and receivable

In this chapter

- Accounts receivable.
- Accounts payable.
- Managing foreign trades.

Accounts receivable

> Need to balance improved sales
> and profit against the costs
> of allowing credit.

Factors influencing credit policies

- Demand for products.
- Risk of irrecoverable debts.
- Financing costs.
- Industry norms and competitors' terms.
- Cost of credit control.

Assessing creditworthiness

Assessing customer's credit risk.

Companies need to assess the creditworthiness of all customers – new customers immediately and all customers periodically. Sources of information are:

- bank

- trade references
- published information
- credit agencies
- company's own sales record.

Control credit limits

Set limits for both the amount of credit offered and the time taken to repay.

Key Point

It is important to monitor orders as well as invoiced sales before extending credit further.

Invoice promptly and collect overdue debts

An effective administration system for receivables must be established. It is essential to invoice promptly and to act quickly should a debt go overdue.

Follow-up procedures

The longer a debt is overdue the greater the risk of default.

Reminder letter
↓
Telephone calls
↓
Withholding supplies
↓
Debt collectors
↓
Legal action

Monitoring the credit system

This is an essential part of working capital management as is taking corrective action when required.

- Age analysis.
- Ratios.
- Statistical data.

Financial implications of offering credit

Cost of financing receivables is the interest cost.

Interest cost = Receivable balance x Interest (overdraft) rate

Receivable balance = receivables days × annual sales / 365
(or 360 if specified in the question)

Discounts

Cash discounts are given to encourage early payment by customers. The cost of the discount (i.e. less cash received from customers) is balanced against the savings the company receives from a lower balance (and therefore a lower receivables financing (interest) cost) and a shorter average collecting period. Discounts may also reduce the number of bad debts.

$$\text{Annual cost of the discount} = \left(1 + \frac{\text{discount}}{\text{amount left to pay}}\right)^{\text{no. of periods}} - 1$$

where no. of periods $= \dfrac{365 \,/\, 52 \,/\, 12}{\text{no. of days / weeks / months earlier the money is received}}$

Key Point

The annual cost calculation is based on the amount net of discount.

If the cost of offering the discount is greater than the rate of overdraft interest then the discount should not be offered.

This can be calculated in one of two ways:

Calculate the cost of the discount using the formula and compare it to the overdraft rate

Or

Calculate the annual reduction in cash received from customers who take the discount and compare it to the receivables funding (interest) cost saved from the reduction in the receivables balance.

Invoice discounting

Definition

Invoice discounting is a method of raising finance against the security of receivables without using the sales ledger administration services of a factor.

- Temporary source of finance.
- Repayable when the debt is cleared.
- Confidential service.

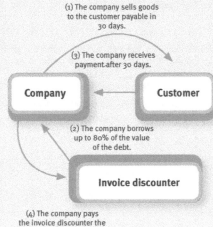

(1) The company sells goods to the customer payable in 30 days.

(3) The company receives payment after 30 days.

Company

Customer

(2) The company borrows up to 80% of the value of the debt.

Invoice discounter

(4) The company pays the invoice discounter the amount borrowed plus interest.

Factoring

Factoring is the outsourcing of the credit control department to a third party. The company can choose some or all of the following three services offered by the factor:

1. debt collection and administration (recourse or non-recourse)

2. financing

3. credit insurance.

Administration and debt collection only

(1) The company sells goods to the customer payable in 30 days.

Company → **Customer**

(2) The company sells the debt to the factor. The factor administers the sale ledger.

(4) The factor pays the company less an administration fee.

Factor

(3) The customer pays the factor after 30 days.

Debt Collection and administration with financing

(1) The company sells goods to the customer payable in 30 days.

```
Company  →  Customer
```

(3) Up to 80% of the debt is paid to the company in advance.

(4) The customer pays the factor after 30 days.

```
Factor
```

(2) The company sells the debt to the factor. The factor administers the sale ledger.
(5) The factor pays the company the balance less an administration fee and financing fee.

To evaluate whether factoring or discounts is worthwhile, calculate the revised receivables balance, and hence the revised cost of financing receivables.

Factoring can help in three ways, depending on the level of service provided.

- Administration and debt collection could shorten the payment period and reduced admin costs to the company.
- Advance of money can save having an overdraft (although it will not necessarily be cheaper than an overdraft).
- Non-recourse factoring can eliminate irrecoverable debts – but may be expensive.

Accounts payable

> Balance this free source of finance against loss of supplier goodwill and possible increase in prices.

Key Point

By delaying payment to payables companies face possible problems.

- Supplier may refuse to supply in future.

- Supplier may only supply on a cash basis.

- Loss of reputation.

- Supplier may increase price in future.

Discounts

Suppliers may offer discounts to encourage early settlement.

The benefit of the discount in terms of the lower cash value paid to the supplier needs to be compared with the additional interest cost resulting from a lower payables balance (and therefore a higher overdraft balance needed to compensate for the reduction in the free source of finance).

This is the same technique as is used for assessing whether to offer settlement discounts to customers (see accounts receivable section) but from the opposite point of view – now the business is the customer instead of the supplier.

Managing foreign trades

Key Point

Additional risks that are incurred with overseas receivables and payables are export credit risk and foreign transaction exposure.

Definition

Export credit risk is the risk of failure or delay in collecting payments due from foreign customers.

Possible causes of export credit risk

- Insolvent companies.
- Political risk.
- Bank failure.
- Unconvertible currencies.

Possible solutions to export credit risk

- Using banks as intermediaries.
- ILC – Irrevocable letter of credit.
- Acquiring guarantees.
- Taking out export cover.
- Good business management.

Exam focus

Recent FM (previously known as F9) exams to include a question on accounts receivable include:

- June 2010 – ZSE Co
- December 2010 – WQZ Co
- December 2013 – Plot Co
- June 2015 – Widnor Co
- Sep / Dec 2015 – ZXC Co
- September 2016 – Nesud Co
- Mar / Jun 2017 – Pangli Co
- Sep / Dec 2018 – Oscar Co

10

Working capital management – cash and funding strategies

In this chapter

- Holding cash.
- Cash management.
- Short-term investment.
- Financing working capital.

Holding cash

Organisations that have insufficient cash to pay their liabilities promptly can lose settlement discounts, goodwill and potentially be forced into liquidation.

Key Point

The reasons for holding cash are:

* transactions motive
* precautionary motive
* investment motive.

Key Point

Again we have the balancing act between liquidity and profitability (returns on invested cash).

Cash management

Cash management models have been developed in an attempt to minimise the cost of moving funds between current accounts and short-term investments.

The Miller-Orr Model

A model for setting the target cash balance which incorporates uncertainty in the cash inflows and outflows.

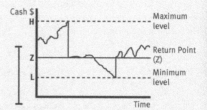

Lower limit set by management. Upper limit = lower limit + spread

Return point = Lower limit + ($\frac{1}{3}$ x spread)

Spread = $3[(\frac{3}{4}$ x Transaction cost x Variance of cash flows$) \div$ Interest rate $]^{\frac{1}{3}}$

Note: variance and interest rates should be expressed in daily terms.

Variance = standard deviation^2

The Baumol Model

EOQ inventory model used to establish the value of cash to be transferred between the current account and an investment account when the demand for cash is moving steadily on one direction.

$$Q = \sqrt{\frac{2C_oD}{C_h}}$$

Where C_o = transaction costs (brokerage, commission, etc.)

D = demand for cash over the period

C_h = cost of holding cash

Q = the amount of money to transfer between current and short-term investment accounts.

The model suggests that cash held in non-interest bearing accounts should be low when interest rates are high.

Cash forecasts

An estimate of cash receipts and payments for a future period under existing conditions.

Forecasts can be prepared from planned receipts and payments, balance sheet predictions or working capital ratios.

Cash budgets

A cash budget is a commitment to a plan for cash receipts and payments for a future period after taking any action necessary to bring the forecast into line with the overall business plan.

Cash budget – prepared as part of the annual master budget.

Cash forecast – prepared continually throughout the year to monitor and manage cashflows.

Key Point

Remember that cash flow forecasts and budgets deal with cash and not accounting flows.

Pro forma for a cash budget

	1	2	3	4
	$	$	$	$
Receipts (Few lines)				
Sub-total (A)	—	—	—	—
	—	—	—	—
Payments (Many lines) Sub-total (B)				
Net cash flow (A – B)	—	—	—	—
Bal brought forward	—	—	—	—
Bal carried forward				

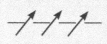

Short-term investment

Profitability
- Favourable rates? Fixed or variable interest rate?
- Currency?
- Tax implications?
- Term to maturity?
- Forecasts' accuracy?

Choosing short-term investments

Liquidity
- Penalties for early withdrawal?
- Availability of bridging finance?
- Time period?
- Alterations in returns for differing time periods?

Risk
- Would a foreign currency be better for investment?
- Inflationary risk of future spending?

Financing working capital

Traditionally, current assets were financed out of short-term credit whilst non-current assets would be financed by long-term funds (debt or equity).

However, in most businesses a proportion of the current assets are 'permanent'.

The choice of how to finance the permanent current assets is a matter for managerial judgement, but includes an analysis of the costs + risks of short-term finance:

Benefits of short-term finance	Problems with short-term finance
• Usually cheaper • More flexible	• Renewal problems • Risk due to changing interest rates

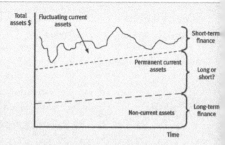

Approaches to the management of working capital

- **Aggressive approach**

  Finance all fluctuating current assets and most permanent current assets with short-term finance.

- **Conservative approach**

  Long-term finance is used for most current assets including a proportion of fluctuating current assets.

- **Matching approach**

  Fluctuating current assets financed out of short-term credit; permanent current assets and non-current assets financed by long-term funds.

Aggressive

- Short-term finance is usually cheaper than long-term finance.
- The lower financing costs should result in better profitability.
- Quicker cash turnover may allow more reinvestment and hence allow the business to expand more quickly.
- High risk strategy due to renewal problems.

Conservative

- Lower liquidity risk.
- Greater ability to meet a sudden surge in sales demand.
- More relaxed credit policy for receivables may improve sales.
- More expensive.

Note

Generally, the more conservative the approach, the lower the risk, but the higher the cost in terms of money tied up in working capital.

Exam focus

Recent FM (previously known as F9) exams to cover cash management include:

- June 2013 – TGA Co
- June 2014 – CSZ Co
- December 2014 – Flit Co
- Mar / Jun 2017 – Pangli Co
- Sep / Dec 2019 – Dusty Co
- Mar / Jul 2020 – Pumice Co

The economic environment for business

In this chapter

- Macro economic policy.
- Macro economic policy and the business sector.
- Government intervention and regulation.
- Corporate governance.

Macro economic policy

Definition

Macro economic policy is the management of the economy by government in such a way as to influence the performance and behaviour of the economy as a whole.

Principal objectives

Full employment of resources.

Price stability.

Economic growth.

Balance of payments equilibrium.

An appropriate distribution of income and wealth.

Note: There will be trade-offs in the pursuit of these objectives.

Macro economic policy and the business sector

Macroeconomic policy

Maintain stable aggregate demand

Helps business plan:

- investment
- employment
- output

Influence costs

Methods include:

Exchange rates

Fiscal policy: taxation

Monetary policy: Interest rates

Monetary policy is concerned with influencing the overall monetary conditions in the economy in particular:

- the volume of money in circulation – the money supply

- the price of money – interest rates.

Fiscal policy is the manipulation of the government spending, taxation and borrowing in order to influence the level of aggregate demand and therefore the level of activity in the economy.

Public expenditure = taxes raised + government borrowing (+ sundry other income).

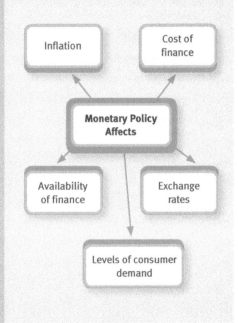

Taxation – main source of government spending.

- Direct taxation – tax on income.
- Indirect taxation – tax on consumption.

Government borrowing

- Short-term e.g. Treasury Bills.
- Long-term e.g. National Savings Certificates.

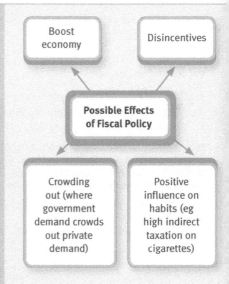

Boost economy

Disincentives

Possible Effects of Fiscal Policy

Crowding out (where government demand crowds out private demand)

Positive influence on habits (eg high indirect taxation on cigarettes)

Government intervention and regulation

In addition to fiscal and monetary policies, governments can also:

- impose pricing restrictions when a market lacks competition

- have public provision of activities (e.g. nationalisation)

- control monopolies either via legislation and/or prevention

- regulate pricing and competition in some industries, particularly utilities

- regulate to affect business activities (e.g. green legislation) in other ways or provide a framework for self-regulation

- provide assistance either financially via grants or the provision of advice and information.

Corporate governance

Definition

Corporate governance is 'the system by which companies are directed and controlled' and covers issues such as ethics, risk management and stakeholder protection.

Many countries have regulation on:

- separation of the supervisory and the management functions

- transparency in the recruitment and remuneration of the board

- appointment of non-executive directors

- establishment of an audit committee

- establishment of risk control procedures.

12

Financial markets and the treasury function

In this chapter

- The role of financial markets.
- The role of financial institutions.
- Money market instruments.
- The role of the treasury function.

'The financial system' is an umbrella term covering the following:

- Financial markets – e.g. stock exchanges, money markets.
- Financial institutions – e.g. banks, building societies, insurance companies and pension funds.
- Financial securities – e.g. mortgages, bonds, bills and equity shares.

Collectively the financial system does the following:

(1) Channels funds from lenders to borrowers.

(2) Provides a mechanism for payments – e.g. direct debits, cheque clearing system.

(3) Creates liquidity and money – e.g. banks create money through increasing their lending.

(4) Provides financial services such as insurance and pensions.

(5) Offers facilities to manage investment portfolios – e.g. to hedge risk.

The role of financial markets

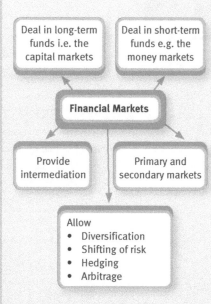

Deal in long-term funds i.e. the capital markets

Deal in short-term funds e.g. the money markets

Financial Markets

Provide intermediation

Primary and secondary markets

Allow
- Diversification
- Shifting of risk
- Hedging
- Arbitrage

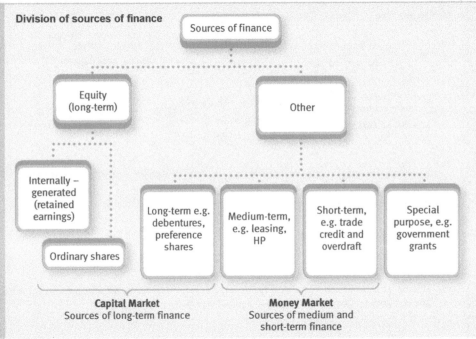

Division of sources of finance

- Sources of finance
  - Equity (long-term)
    - Internally – generated (retained earnings)
    - Ordinary shares
  - Other
    - Long-term e.g. debentures, preference shares
    - Medium-term, e.g. leasing, HP
    - Short-term, e.g. trade credit and overdraft
    - Special purpose, e.g. government grants

Capital Market
Sources of long-term finance

Money Market
Sources of medium and short-term finance

Money markets

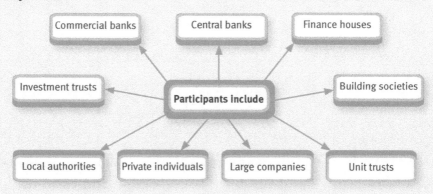

Money markets play a key role in:

- providing short-term liquidity to companies, banks and the public sector
- providing short-term trade finance
- allowing an organisation to manage its exposure to foreign currency risk and interest rate risk (see chapters on foreign exchange and interest rate risk).

The capital markets

The capital markets deal in longer-term finance, mainly via a stock exchange.

The major types of securities dealt on capital markets are as follows:

- public sector and foreign stocks
- company securities (shares and corporate bonds)
- Eurobonds.

International capital markets

- Domestic funds are supplied to a foreign user, or
- Foreign funds are supplied to a domestic user
- The currencies used need not be those of either the lender or the borrower.

The most important international markets are:

- the Euromarkets
- the foreign bond markets.

Eurocurrency is money deposited with a bank outside its country of origin.

Stock markets and corporate bond markets

The role of the stock market

- Facilitate trade in stock and corporate bonds.
- Raise capital for industry.
- Determine a fair price for assets traded.

The role of financial institutions

Definition

Intermediation is the process whereby potential borrowers are brought together with potential lenders by a third party, the intermediary.

Intermediaries

- Clearing banks
- Investment/merchant banks
- Insurance companies
- Finance Houses
- Factors
- Leasing companies
- Investment trusts
- Unit trusts
- Pension funds
- Savings banks
- Building societies

Financial intermediaries have a number of important roles:

- Risk reduction
- Aggregation
- Maturity transformation

Money market instruments

A financial manager needs to understand the characteristics of the following money market instruments:

```
              money market instruments
```

Coupon bearing securities
- CDs
- Repos

Discount securities
- Treasury bills
- Commercial bills
- Commercial paper
- Bankers acceptances

Derivatives
- FRAs
- Caps and floors
- Interest rate futures
- Options on interest rate futures
- Interest rate swaps
- Swaptions

The role of the treasury function

Role of a treasury department:

- banking
- foreign exchange
- cash and currency management
- raising finance
- risk and insurance
- short-term asset investment
- advice on:
  - gearing
  - dividend policy
  - resource allocation
  - mergers and acquisitions
  - currency issues
  - cash management.

The treasury function may be centralised or decentralised.

Exam focus

13

Foreign exchange risk

In this chapter

- Exchange rate systems.
- Types of currency risk.
- Changes in exchange rates.
- Managing foreign currency risk.

Exchange rate systems

- Floating exchange rates – freely or managed.

- Fixed exchange rates.

Definition

An exchange rate is the price of a currency expressed in terms of another currency.

Types of currency risk

Key Point

The foreign exchange risk exposure of companies can be broken down into three categories:

- **transaction exposure**

- **translation** (or accounting) **exposure**

- **economic exposure.**

Definition

Transaction risk is the risk of an exchange rate changing between the transaction date and the subsequent settlement date.

- The impact can be assessed using sensitivity analysis for various different exchange rates.

Definition

Translation exposure is the change in the value of a subsidiary due to changes in exchange rates. This is an accounting risk rather than a cash-based one.

Definition

Economic risk is the variation in the value of the business due to changes in exchange rates causing a loss in competitive strength.

- The expected exchange rates can be predicted and factored into the NPV analysis.

Changes in exchange rates

These result from changes in the demand for and supply of the currency.

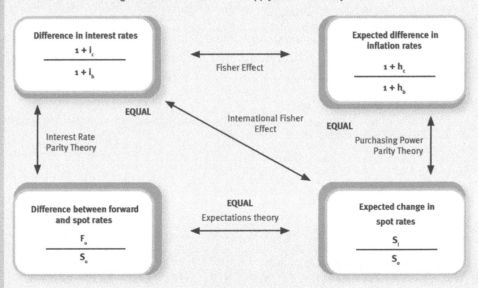

Purchasing power parity theory (PPPT)

Definition

PPPT claims that the rate of exchange between two currencies depends on the relative inflation rates within the respective countries.

Key Point

PPPT predicts that the country with the higher inflation will be subject to a depreciation of its currency.

To estimate future spot rates

$$S_1 = S_0 \times \frac{(1 + h_c)}{(1 + h_b)}$$

where

S_0 = current spot

S_1 = expected future spot

h_b = inflation rate in base country

h_c = inflation rate in other country (counter currency).

Assumptions
- free market
- no barriers to trade
- no transport or transaction costs.

Interest rate parity theory (IRPT)

Definition

The IRPT claims that the difference between the spot and the forward exchange rates is equal to the differential between interest rates available in the two currencies.

The forward rate is a future exchange rate, agreed now, for buying or selling an amount of currency on an agreed future date.

Key Point

The IRPT predicts that the country with the higher interest rate will see its forward rate depreciate. What an investor gains by investing in a currency with a higher interest rate, must be lost when changing the investment back into the home currency.

To calculate the current forward rate for one year's time

$$F_0 = S_0 \times \frac{(1 + i_c)}{(1 + i_b)}$$

where

F_0 = forward rate

i_b = interest rate in base currency

i_c = interest rate in counter currency

S_0 = current spot rate

The same assumptions apply as for PPPT.

Expectations theory

Definition

The expectations theory states that the current forward rate is an unbiased predictor of the spot rate at that point in the future.

The International Fisher Effect

Definition

This states that the interest rate differentials between two countries provide an unbiased predictor of future changes in the spot rate of exchange.

Managing foreign currency risk

Taking measures to eliminate or reduce a risk is called:

- hedging the risk or
- hedging the exposure.

Practical approaches

- Invoice in home currency and pay for all imports in home currency.
- Do nothing – bear the risk.
- Leading – changing currency early if it is estimated that that will be advantageous.
- Lagging – changing currency as late as possible if it is estimated that that will be advantageous.
- Matching inflows and outflows in the foreign currency.
- Use foreign currency bank accounts.

Trading in currencies

The foreign exchange market is an international market in which national currencies are traded.

Exchange rate spread

Exchange rates are expressed with a counter and a base currency. For example, the exchange rate between US$ and GB£ may be expressed as $1.4325 – $1.4330 = £1

The currency with a value of 1, here £, is known as the base currency. The other currency, here $, is the counter currency.

The two $ values represent the exchange rate spread, a buy price and a sell price. To work out which is which:

The **lower** rate, $1.4325, is the rate at which the bank will **sell** the ($) **counter** currency in exchange for the (£) base currency (the bank **sells low**).

The **higher** rate, \$1.4330, is the rate at which the bank will **buy** the (\$) **counter** currency in exchange for the (£) base currency (the bank **buys high**).

Key Point

Remember that the bank will always trade at the rate that is more favourable to itself.

The difference between the bid and offer prices is known as the 'spread'. It represents the transactions costs and profits of the dealer in the currency.

Depreciation and appreciation of a currency

When one currency depreciates against another, the other currency will appreciate.

For instance, if an exchange rate between US\$ and GB £ moves from US\$1.5 = £1 to US\$1.4 = £1 the £ has depreciated against the \$ (it can now buy fewer \$ than before) and the \$ has appreciated against the £ (fewer \$ are needed to buy £s).

Hedging with forward contracts

Definition

The **spot market** is where you can buy and sell a currency now (immediate delivery).

The **forward market** is where you can buy and sell a currency, at a fixed future date for a predetermined rate i.e. the forward rate of exchange. Quoted as a margin on the spot.

Advantages include:

- Flexibility with regard to the amount.
- Relatively straightforward.

Disadvantages include:

- Contractual commitment that must be completed on the due date.
- No opportunity to benefit from favourable exchange movements.

A money market hedge

Instead of hedging a currency exposure with a forward contract, a company could use the money markets to lend or borrow, and achieve a similar result.

To hedge a payment:

- Buy the present value of the foreign currency amount today at the spot rate (this is an immediate payment in sterling and may involve borrowing the funds).
- Place the foreign currency on deposit where it will accrue interest until the settlement date.
- Use the deposit to make the foreign currency payment on the settlement date.

To hedge a receipt:

- Borrow the present value of the foreign currency amount today. This is then translated at the spot rate giving an immediate receipt in sterling which can be invested.
- The foreign loan accrues interest until the transaction date.
- The loan is then repaid with the foreign currency receipt.

Hedging with futures

Futures are like forward contracts but are for standardised amounts and can therefore be traded on currency exchanges.

Hedging with options

Options give the right but not the obligation to buy or sell a currency at some point in the future at a predetermined rate. The option therefore eliminates downside risk but allows participation in the upside.

Options may be:

PUT   **CALL**

Right to sell currency   Right to buy currency

The additional flexibility comes at a price – a premium must be paid to purchase an option, whether or not it is ever used.

Exam focus

Recent FM (previously known as F9) exams covering foreign exchange risk include:

- Jue 2014 – CSZ Co
- December 2014 – PZK Co
- June 2015 – Rose Co
- Sep / Dec 2015 – GXJ Co
- Mar / Jun 2016 – Plam Co
- September 2016 – Herd Co
- December 2016 – Park Co
- Mar / Jun 2019 – Peony Co

14

Interest rate risk

In this chapter

- The yield curve.
- Hedging interest rate risk.

Definition

Interest rate risk is the risk of incurring losses due to adverse movements in interest rates.

Exposures to interest rate risk can be hedged. There are several methods of hedging the risk. These include the use of:

- Forward rate agreements (FRAs).
- Interest rate futures.
- Interest rate options.
- Interest rate swaps.

Definition

Basis risk is the interest rate exposure which is not eliminated by a hedge.

The yield curve (Also known as the term structure of interest rates.)

A relationship between interest rates and the time to maturity. It is normally accepted that

the longer the period to maturity for a debt, the greater the yield or return that the debt must offer. A debt that matures after many years has more risk associated with it then one maturing soon, so lenders require a higher yield.

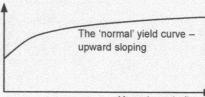

The gross redemption yield reflects the overall return earned from holding the debt including the interest yield together with the eventual redemption value. The years to maturity may be plotted many years in advance.

Factors affecting the shape of the yield curve

1 Liquidity preference.
2 Expectation (of interest rate movements).
3 Market Segmentation.

Implications of the yield curve

Short term finance is usually cheaper than longer term finance. E.g. instead of a fixed rate 10 yr loan it should be cheaper to get a 5 yr loan followed by another 5 yr loan. Unfortunately there will be additional administration costs and there is the risk that interest rates will have increased making the second loan more expensive.

Hedging interest rate risk

Forward Rate Agreements (FRAs)

Definition

A forward rate agreement (FRA) for interest rates is a financial instrument that can be used to fix the interest rate on a loan or deposit starting at a date in the future.

- When an FRA reaches its settlement date, the buyer and seller must settle the contract.
- For a deposit, the company will be the seller of the FRA and for a borrowing, the company will be the buyer, with the bank fulfilling the opposite role.
- If, on the date of a deposit, the pre-agreed FRA rate is higher than the deposit rate, the FRA provider will make a cash payment for the difference to the depositor. If the FRA rate is below the deposit rate, the depositor will instead pay the difference to the FRA provider.
- For loans, the FRA provider pays out the difference when the loan rate is higher than the FRA rate and receives the difference from the borrower if the rate position is reversed.

Terminology

A 2-5 FRA at 5.00 – 4.70 means:

- The agreement starts in 2 months' time and ends in 5 months' time.
- The rate for borrowing is 5.00% (the higher rate).
- The rate for lending (investing) is 4.70%.

Definition

An **Interest Rate Guarantee (IRG)** is an option on an FRA and protects the company from adverse movements whilst allowing it to take advantage of favourable movements. Their flexibility means they are more expensive than FRAs – used when unsure as to which way interest rates will move.

Interest rate futures

Definition

Interest rate futures are standardised exchange-traded contracts agreed now between buyers and sellers, for settlement at a future date.

There are two broad types of interest rate futures.

- Short-term interest rate futures (STIRs).
- Bond futures.

A futures contract is a promise, e.g. if you sell a futures contract you have sold the promise to make interest payments.

The borrowing is notional.

- The position is 'closed out' by reversing the original deal. The two contracts then cancel each other out.
- The only cash flow that arises is the net interest paid or received ie. the profit or loss on the futures contract.

Interest rate swaps

Definition

An interest rate swap is an agreement between parties to swap a floating rate stream of interest payments for a fixed steam of interest payments and vice versa. They can be used to:

- hedge against adverse movements in interest rates
- to obtain cheaper finance.

Exam focus

Recent FM (previously known as F9) exams to contain questions on interest rate risk include:

- December 2013 – Spot Co
- June 2015 – Rose Co
- Sep / Dec 2015 – GXJ Co
- Mar / Jun 2016 – Plam Co
- September 2016 – Herd Co
- December 2016 – Park Co
- Mar / Jun 2019 – Peony Co

15

Sources of finance

In this chapter

- Short-term sources of finance.
- Long-term finance.
- Finance for small and medium enterprises.

Factors affecting choice of finance:

- Cost
- Duration
- Term structure of interest rates
- Gearing
- Accessibility
- Control
- Security
- Cashflow

Short-term sources of finance

- Bank loans
- Bank overdrafts
- Leasing
- Working capital

Leasing

Definition

A lease is a contract between a lessor and a lessee for the hire of a particular asset in return for specified rentals.

Leases may be:

(a) Short-term

For leases less than 12 months in duration.

(b) Long-term

For leases with a term of more than 12 months, unless the underlying asset is of low value, the asset is capitalised and the lease liability recognised. In essence, similar to purchasing the asset with the use of long-term finance

Long-term finance

Equity

- Owning a share confers part ownership of the business.

- Shareholders have full rights to participate in the business through voting in general meetings.

Preference shares (non-equity)

- Pays a fixed dividend, ranking before (in preference to) ordinary shareholders.
- Unsecured, but on liquidation of the company are repaid before equity.
- Hybrid form of finance ranking between Debt and Equity for payment.
- For gearing purposes, usually considered to be debt.
- Dividends are cumulative unless otherwise stated.
- Not very popular, it is the worst of both worlds i.e.
  - it is not tax efficient
  - it offers no opportunity for high dividends when the company is doing well as investors receive a fixed return.

Finance leases – note split into primary and secondary period.

Debt

- Bank finance
- Bonds (traded investments)

Definition

A **debenture** is a written acknowledgement of a debt by a company and normally contains provisions as to the payment of interest and the terms of repayment of principal.

Features

- Interest is paid out of pre-tax profits as an expense of the business.
- Cheaper for the company than equity because it is cheaper to arrange, interest payments usually lower than dividends (because less risky to investor) and the interest attracts tax relief.
- It carries a risk of default if interest and principal payments are not met, so the debt-holder can force the company into liquidation.

- No rights to share in the profits if the company is very successful.

- In the event of default the lender will be able to take assets in exchange of the amounts owing.

- May be redeemable or irredeemable, secured or unsecured.

- Security can be by fixed or floating charges.

- Market rates of bonds will fluctuate, depending on the prevailing interest rates.

Hybrids – convertibles

- Have elements of equity and debt.

- Give the holder the right to convert to other securities (generally ordinary shares) at either a predetermined price or ratio.

- Provide immediate finance at low cost.

- Has the effect of giving the debt holder a potential capital gain over and above the return from the debt interest.

- If the value of the shares is greater than that of the debt on the exercise date then conversion will be made by the investor. If share value is lower than the debt value the investor may retain the debt to maturity.

Hybrids – Warrants

- An option to buy shares at a specified point in the future for a specified (exercise) price.

- The warrant offers a potential capital gain where the share price may rise above the exercise price.

- The holder has the option to buy the share.

- The warrant has many uses including:

  - as additional consideration when issuing debt to make it more attractive

  - as a means of offering incentives to staff.

Venture capital

This is the provision of risk bearing capital to companies with high growth potential – generally start-up and late stage growth finance for small companies.

1 It is high risk investment –venture capitalists are not investing in listed companies.

2 It is not passive portfolio investment but involves a close working relationship between the venture capital company and the company receiving the funds.

3 Medium-term investment. The venture capital company will be hoping to realise the equity shares it has acquired at a

profit in five or so years after it first purchased the shares (the exit). It is hoping that either the company will go public or the shares will be bought by another company or by other shareholders.

4 The venture capitalist will have an exit strategy in place before investing in shares.

Retained earnings

The single most important source of finance. Most businesses use retained earnings as the basis of their financing needs.

New share issues

- Placing

- Offer for sale

- Offer for sale by tender

- Intermediaries' offer

- Rights issue

- Sometimes governments encourage equity investment in start-up companies. In the UK there is the Enterprise Investment Scheme.

Methods of obtaining a listing

There are three main methods of obtaining a quotation on the Stock Exchange:

1 offer for sale

2 placing

3 stock exchange introduction.

Rights issues

Existing shareholders have the right to subscribe to new share issues in proportion to their existing holdings, thus enabling them to retain their existing share of voting rights.

Theoretical Ex-rights price (TERP)

The new share price after the issue is known as the theoretical ex-rights price and is calculated by finding the weighted average of the old price and the rights price, weighted by the number of shares.

$$TERP = \frac{\text{Market capitalisation before the issue} + \text{Proceeds from the issue}}{\text{Total number of shares in issue after the issue}}$$

Value of a right = Ex-rights price – Issue price

Value of a right per existing share = Value of a right / number of shares needed to earn one right

Shareholders' options

The shareholders' options with a rights issue are to:

1 take up his rights

2 renounce his rights and sell them in the market

3 renounce part of his rights and take up the remainder

4 do nothing.

Finance for small and medium enterprises

There is a funding gap for many SMEs which arises when they want to expand beyond their means of finance but are not yet ready for a listing on the Stock Exchange or the Alternative Investment Market.

Small firms are also considered more risky.

The financial investors

* Banks, but they are reluctant to invest heavily in SMEs due to lack of security and being risk averse.

* Venture capitalists who provide risk-bearing capital to companies with high growth potential.

* Business angels – wealthy individuals investing in start-up, early stage or expanding firms, at lower levels than a venture capitalist.

Government solutions

Government policies to

Increase the marketability of shares e.g. small firm markets

Offer tax incentives for investors:
e.g. EIS, VCT, employee share schemes

Provide assistance:
– business links
– financial assistance

Key Point

Islamic finance

Interest (riba) is strictly prohibited within Islamic finance. Instead interest is replaced with cash flows from productive sources, such as returns from wealth generating investment activities.

In an Islamic bank, the money provided by depositers is not lent, but is instead channeled into an underlying investment activity, which will earn profit. The depositer is rewarded by a share in that profit, after a management fee is deducted by the bank.

Key terms in Islamic finance include:

– Murabaha (trade credit)

– Ijara (lease finance)

– Sukuk (debt finance)

– Mudaraba (equity finance)

– Musharaka (venture capital).

Exam focus

Recent FM (previously known as F9) exams covering sources of finance include:

- December 2011 – Bar Co
- June 2013 – GXG Co
- December 2013 – Spot Co
- June 2014 – MFZ Co
- December 2014 – Tinep Co
- June 2015 – Grenarp Co
- Mar / Jun 2016 – Dinla Co
- December 2016 – Gadner Co
- Mar / Jun 2018 – Tin Co
- Mar / Jun 2019 – Tulip Co
- Mar / Jun 2019 – Corfe Co
- Mar / Jul 2020 – LaForge Co

16

Dividend Policy

In this chapter

- The dividend decision.

The dividend decision

Is shareholders' wealth affected by a company's dividend policy?

Dividend irrelevancy theory

Shareholders do not mind how their returns are split between dividends and capital gains assuming perfect capital markets and no taxation.

Residual theory

Dividends are important but the pattern of them is not.

Provided the present values of the future cashflows remains the same, the timing of the payment is irrelevant.

Recognising the costs involved in raising new finance this theory concludes that only after investing is all positive NPV projects should a dividend be paid.

This theory still assumes no taxation and no market imperfections.

Dividend relevance

In the real world market imperfections mean that:

- dividend signalling may occur (reductions in dividends can be seen as bad news)
- changes in dividend policy may conflict with shareholder liquidity requirements
- the clientele effect – investors chose companies as part of their tax planning.

Companies tend to adopt a stable dividend policy and keep investors informed of changes.

Other influences on company dividend policy are:

- liquidity
- legal restrictions
- debt covenants.

Chapter 16

Alternatives to dividends

- Share repurchase.

- Scrip dividends (bonus shares) – firms offering shareholders extra shares instead of cash.

Recent FM (previously known as F9) exams to cover the dividend decision include:

- December 2010 – NN Co.

- Mar / Jul 2020 – LaForge Co

The cost of capital

In this chapter

- The dividend valuation model.
- The cost of debt.
- WACC.
- Risk and return.
- CAPM.

The dividend valuation model

The dividend valuation model states that the current share price is determined by the future dividends, discounted at the investors' required rate of return.

Constant Dividend

$$P_o = \frac{d}{r_e} \qquad r_e = \frac{d}{P_o}$$

Where:

r_e = the cost of equity

P_0 = the ex-dividend market price of the share

d = the constant dividend

- Note that r_e and k_e are used interchangeably to represent the cost of equity

Growth

The dividend valuation model with constant growth

$$P_o = \frac{d_1}{(r_e - g)} \qquad r_e = \frac{d_1}{P_o} + g$$

Where:

g = a constant rate of growth in dividends

d_1 = dividend to be paid in one year's time

This can also be written as

$$r_e = \frac{d_0(1 + g)}{P_0} + g$$

where d_0 = dividend just paid

There are 2 main methods of determining growth:

1 The averaging method

$$g = \sqrt[n]{\frac{\text{current dividend}}{\text{dividend n years ago}}} - 1$$

2 Gordon's growth model

$$g = br_e$$

where r_e = accounting rate of return

   b = proportion of funds retained

Key Point

Assumptions of the DVM

- Dividends will be paid in perpetuity.

- Dividends are constant or growing at a fixed rate.

- The cost of equity is larger than the growth rate

The cost of debt

Kp the cost of preference shares

For irredeemable preference shares:

$$K_p = \frac{d}{P_o}$$

Kd the cost of debt

Key Point

- Be careful to distinguish between the company's perspective (net of tax relief on interest payments; $K_d(1 - T)$) and the lenders' perspective (pre-tax; K_d).

- The market value of debt is always quoted in $100 nominal units or blocks.

- Do not confuse the coupon rate with the cost of debt.

Calculations

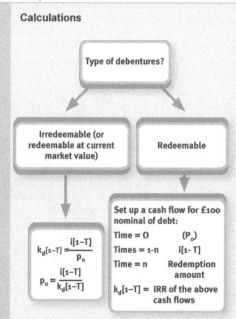

Type of debentures?

Irredeemable (or redeemable at current market value)

Redeemable

$$k_{d[1-T]} = \frac{i[1-T]}{P_o}$$

$$P_o = \frac{i[1-T]}{k_{d[1-T]}}$$

Set up a cash flow for £100 nominal of debt:

Time = 0	(P_o)
Times = 1-n	$i[1-T]$
Time = n	Redemption amount

$k_{d[1-T]}$ = IRR of the above cash flows

Where:

i = the pre-tax interest paid on $100 nominal of debt

T = tax rate

P_o = ex-interest market value of $100 nominal of debt.

Note: if you do not know the market value of redeemable debt, then calculate it using the dividend valuation model from the lenders' perspective (you would be given the lender's required rate of return from debt).

MV = PV of future interest and redemption payments discounted at the lenders' required return.

Convertible debt is treated as redeemable debt except the redemption value is the higher of the cash redemption and the future share price if converted. This value is known as its formula value.

Non-traded debt

Cost to company = interest rate x (1 – tax rate).

WACC

In order to provide a discount rate for evaluating projects, the cost of the pool of funds is required.

This is variously referred to as the combined or weighted average cost of capital (WACC).

The funds are used, partly in existing operations and partly to finance new projects. There is not normally any tracing of funds from different sources to their application in specific projects: funds go into a pool of finance.

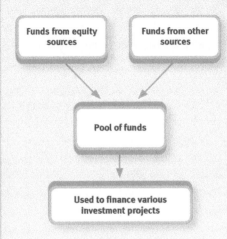

Procedure for calculating the WACC

Step 1 Calculate weights for each source of capital – when possible use the market values.

Step 2 Estimate the cost of each source of capital.

Step 3 Multiply the proportion of the total of each source of capital by the cost of that source of capital.

Step 4 Sum the results of step 3 to give the weighted average cost of capital.

$$WACC = \left[\frac{V_e}{V_e + V_d} \right] k_e + \left[\frac{V_d}{V_e + V_d} \right] k_d (1 - T)$$

k_e = cost of equity

$k_d (1 - T)$ = cost of debt (post tax)

V_e = market value of equity

V_d = market value of debt

Exam focus

When calculating a WACC on a spreadsheet, you may wish to use the following method:

Construct a table with a row for each source of finance. Enter a column for the value weightings (either market values or nominal values, whichever is required by the question). You will also need a column for the costs, which you will calculate as workings. Then enter a column that multiplies, for each source of finance, its weighting by its cost.

The WACC is then calculated as the total of the 'weightings × cost' column divided by the total of the weightings column.

Risk and return

The risk-free rate (Rf) is the minimum rate required by investors for an investment whose returns are certain.

R_f is given in exams as the return on Treasury bills.

The required return on risky securities = risk-free rate + risk premium

CAPM

CAPM can be used to calculate a risk adjusted cost of equity.

Systematic and unsystematic risk

CAPM recognises that total risk comprises:

- systematic risk and
- unsystematic risk.

CAPM uses the ß value of a share to measure its systematic risk and from that predicts the return an investor should require.

The higher an investment's ß, the higher a return an investor will require to compensate him for the risk.

Unsystematic risk can be diversified away by holding more securities as the random good and bad events occurring in companies which make up the portfolio will tend to cancel out to give a more stable, less risky performance:

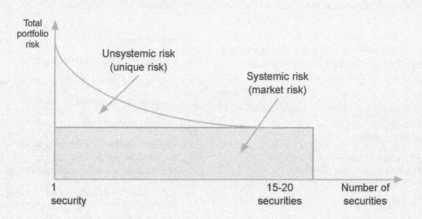

Key Point

The risk-free security – This carries no risk and therefore no systematic risk. The risk-free security hence has a beta of zero.

The market portfolio – This represents the ultimate in diversification and therefore contains only systematic risk.

- The beta of the market portfolio is = 1
- A beta greater than one indicates a riskier than average portfolio
- A beta less than 1 indicates returns less volatile than the market.

The formula for CAPM is

$$E(r_j) = R_f + \beta_j (E(r_m) - R_f)$$

Where:

$E(r_j)$ is the required return from the investment

R_f is the risk free rate of return

β_j is the beta value of the investment

$E(r_m)$ is the expected return from the market portfolio.

Assumptions of CAPM

- A perfect capital market.
- Unrestricted borrowing or lending at the risk-free rate of interest.
- Investors already have a well-diversified portfolio so that their unsystematic risk has been diversified away.
- Uniformity of investor expectations.
- All forecasts are made in the context of one time period only.

Advantages of the CAPM

- It provides a market based relationship between risk and return, by making an assessment of security risk and predicting the rate of return given that risk.

- It shows why only systematic risk is important in this relationship.

- It is one of the best methods of estimating a quoted company's cost of equity capital.

- It provides a basis for establishing risk adjusted discount rates for capital investment projects.

Limitations of the CAPM

- By concentrating only on systematic risk, other aspects of risk are excluded.

- The model considers only the level of return as being important to investors and not the way in which that return is received. Hence, dividends and capital gains are deemed equally desirable.

- It is strictly a one-period model and should be used with caution, if at all, in the appraisal of multi-period projects.

- Assumes perfect markets.

Exam focus

Recent FM (previously known as F9) exams covering the cost of capital include:

- December 2011 – Close Co
- June 2012 – Corhig Co
- June 2013 – AMH Co
- December 2013 – Card Co
- June 2014 – Fence Co
- December 2014 – Tinep Co
- Sep / Dec 2015 – KQK Co
- Mar / Jun 2016 – Dinla Co
- December 2016 – Gadner Co
- Sep-Dec 2017 – Tufa Co
- Mar / Jun 2019 – Tulip Co
- Mar / Jun 2019 – Corfe Co

18

Capital structure

In this chapter

- Operating gearing.
- Financial gearing.
- Capital structure: The key question.
- Traditional view.
- Modigliani and Miller's view – 1958 – no tax position.
- Modigliani and Miller's view – 1963 – with tax.
- Gearing levels in practice.
- Pecking order theory.
- Using CAPM in project appraisal.

Business risks

Financial gearing ⟷ Operating gearing

Trade-off

Operating gearing

1　Looking at the cost structure (cause)

　Operating gearing　= fixed costs/total costs

or

　　　　　　　= fixed costs/variable costs

2　Looking at the impact on the profit and loss account (effect)

　Operating gearing　= $\dfrac{\text{\% change in EBIT}}{\text{\% change in turnover}}$

or Contribution / PBIT

High operating gearing increases the level of business risk, and is largely due to the industry in which a firm operates.

Financial gearing

A measure of the extent to which debt is used in the capital structure.

Two measures: capital gearing, and interest cover.

Equity gearing

Equity Gearing = $\dfrac{\text{Preference share capital plus long-term debt}}{\text{Ordinary share capital and reserves}}$

Total or capital gearing

Total Gearing = $\dfrac{\text{Preference share capital plus long-term debt}}{\text{Total long-term capital}}$

The ratios can be calculated using either book or market values of debt and equity.

Interest gearing

A profit and loss account measure that considers the ability of the business to cover the cost of debt as it falls due.

$$\text{Interest gearing} = \frac{\text{Debt interest + preference dividends}}{\text{Operating profits before debt interest and tax}}$$

Key Point

The higher the financial gearing the greater the variability of returns to shareholders and the higher the risk.

Capital structure: The key question

Can the directors of a company increase shareholder wealth simply by changing the capital structure?

This is answered by looking at how changing the gearing level affects the company WACC – a lower WACC should result in a more valuable company.

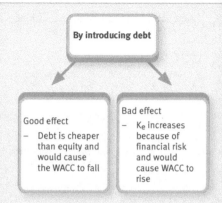

By introducing debt

Good effect
- Debt is cheaper than equity and would cause the WACC to fall

Bad effect
- K_e increases because of financial risk and would cause WACC to rise

There are three views concerning the trade off of these two effects.

1 Traditional view – there is an optimal gearing level, which a firm needs to find by trial and error.

2   Modigliani and Miller (without tax) –
    gearing does not affect shareholder
    wealth.

3   Modigliani and Miller (with tax) – firms
    should gear up as much as possible to
    make use of the tax relief that is available
    on interest payments, but which is not
    available on dividends.

Traditional view

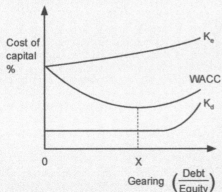

Optimal capital structure

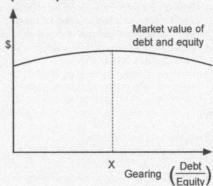

The traditional view therefore claims that
there is an optimal capital structure where
the weighted average cost of capital is at
a minimum. This is at point X in the above
diagrams. At this point the value of the
company is maximised.

Firms should seek to find this level through trial and error. Once achieved, the firm should aim at keeping its gearing level constant. (Note: this is one of the assumptions necessary for using the WACC as a discount rate.)

Modigliani and Miller's view – 1958 – no tax position

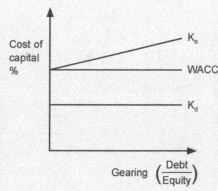

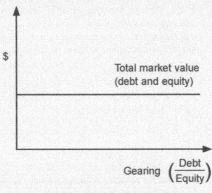

The essential point made by M & M is that, ignoring taxation, a firm should be indifferent between all possible capital structures.

If the weighted average cost of capital is to remain constant at all levels of gearing it follows that any benefit from the use of cheaper debt finance (cheaper because of lower risk) must be exactly offset by the increase in the cost of equity.

The **assumptions** underpinning M&M's theory include:

- No taxation.
- Perfect capital markets.
- Rational investors.
- No transaction costs.
- Debt is risk free.

Modigliani and Miller's view – 1963 – with tax

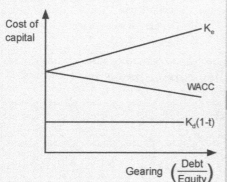

Cost of capital

K_e

WACC

$K_d(1-t)$

Gearing $\left(\dfrac{\text{Debt}}{\text{Equity}}\right)$

As gearing increases, the WACC steadily decreases. Thus firms should seek to gear up as much as possible.

The reason for this is that firms get tax relief on interest paid, making it preferable to pay out interest to investors rather than dividends.

If the other implications of the M & M view are accepted, the introduction of taxation suggests that the higher the level of taxation, the lower the combined cost of capital.

This theory is based on the same assumptions as the original M&M theory with the exception of the no taxation assumption which has now been removed.

Key Point

- Learn the conclusions of the three viewpoints (traditional, M&M without tax and M&M with tax) so you can refer to them in discussion questions.

Gearing levels in practice

Gearing levels tend to based on practical concerns and often follow the industry norm.

Problems with high levels of gearing:

- Bankruptcy risk.
- Agency costs.
- Tax exhaustion.
- Effect on borrowing capacity.
- Risk tolerance of investors may be exceeded.
- Breach of Articles of Association.
- Increases in the cost of borrowing as gearing levels rise.

Pecking order theory

Preferred order for financing is:

- internally generated funds
- debt
- new equity issue.

Key Point

This has implications for investment and gearing levels of firms using the pecking order.

Investment

- The value of a project will alter with the choice of finance for it.

- Choice of finance may impact on the decision to accept or reject a project.

- Higher geared companies with less cash may under-invest.

Gearing

- The higher the cash flow the lower the resultant gearing.

- Equity may be issued at a time of high information asymmetry.

Using CAPM in project appraisal

Use CAPM to calculate the **discount rate** when:

- The project risk is different from that of the company's normal business risk,

  and

- The shareholders of the company are well-diversified.

Projects can be viewed separately from the company undertaking them. All equity-financed projects imply using shareholders' funds to invest in projects which yield shareholder returns via higher dividends. The company that happens to undertake the project is irrelevant, as is its WACC. All that matters for appraisal is the project's cash flows and the project's beta.

CAPM and gearing risk

When using betas in project appraisal, the impact of gearing of the finance used must be borne in mind.

When given, or calculating, betas in the exam it is vital that you are clear what type of beta you have/want.

$ß_e$ = the **Equity Beta**: measures the systematic business risk and the systematic financial risk of a company's shares. Also known as a "geared" beta.

$ß_a$ = the **Asset Beta**: measures the systematic business risk only. Also known as an "un-geared" beta.

The most common exam scenario is where you are given an equity beta but you want an asset beta. To adjust the beta use the following formulae:

$$ß_a = ß_e\left[\frac{V_E}{V_E + V_D\,[1-t]}\right] + ß_d\left[\frac{V_D\,[1-t]}{V_E + V_D\,[1-t]}\right]$$

OR $ß_a = ß_e\left[\dfrac{V_E}{V_E + V_D\,[1-t]}\right]$, where debt is risk-free (as is often assumed)

Note

1   A company's (or project's) equity beta will always be greater than its asset beta, except if there is no gearing, when the two betas will the same.

2   Companies in the same 'area of business' (i.e. same business risk) will have the same asset beta, but

3   Companies in the same area of business will not have the same equity beta unless they also happen to have the same capital structure.

4   If a project is financed by a mix of debt and equity, the returns demanded by equity providers will be higher than if all equity financed (equity beta > asset beta). However, because part of the project is financed by cheap debt, the overall return required is lower than would be required by pure equity financing.

Exam focus

Recent FM (previously known as F9) exams covering capital structure include:

*   June 2012 – Corhig Co
*   June 2013 – AMH Co
*   December 2013 – Card Co
*   June 2015 – Grenarp Co
*   Sep / Dec 2015 – Gemlo Co
*   Sep / Dec 2015 – KQK Co

chapter 19

Financial ratios

In this chapter

- Profitability ratios.
- Debt and gearing ratios.
- Liquidity.
- Investor ratios.
- Potential problems.

Profitability ratios

Key Point

Companies often use measures to assess profitability and/or increase in wealth.

Comparatives and other forms of benchmarking are required if these measures are to be interpreted and the underlying causes investigated.

In isolation, the calculations are meaningless when assessing performance.

Measure	Formula	Use
ROCE	$ROCE = \dfrac{\text{Operating Profit (PBIT)}}{\text{Capital employed}} \times 100$	Measures how much is earned per $1 invested (efficiency)
ROE	ROE (return on equity) = $\dfrac{\text{Profit after tax and after preference dividends}}{\text{Ordinary share capital + reserves}} \times 100$	Measures how much profit a company generates for its ordinary shareholders' investment in the company.
PROFIT MARGINS	Gross profit margin = $\dfrac{\text{Gross profit}}{\text{Revenue}}$ Operating profit margin = $\dfrac{\text{Operating profit}}{\text{Revenue}}$	Measures the return made from each $1 sold

ROCE can be split.

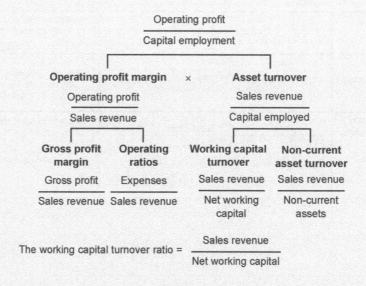

$$\frac{\text{Operating profit}}{\text{Capital employment}}$$

Operating profit margin × **Asset turnover**

$$\frac{\text{Operating profit}}{\text{Sales revenue}}$$

$$\frac{\text{Sales revenue}}{\text{Capital employed}}$$

Gross profit margin	**Operating ratios**	**Working capital turnover**	**Non-current asset turnover**
$\dfrac{\text{Gross profit}}{\text{Sales revenue}}$	$\dfrac{\text{Expenses}}{\text{Sales revenue}}$	$\dfrac{\text{Sales revenue}}{\text{Net working capital}}$	$\dfrac{\text{Sales revenue}}{\text{Non-current assets}}$

$$\text{The working capital turnover ratio} = \frac{\text{Sales revenue}}{\text{Net working capital}}$$

Debt and gearing ratios

In addition to the ratios in chapter 16:

$$\text{Interest cover} = \frac{\text{PBIT}}{\text{Interest}}$$

Liquidity

All of the liquidity ratios were covered in chapter 7.

Debt holder ratios

$$\text{Simple Interest Yield} = \frac{\text{Interest paid (\$) per annum}}{\text{Current Market Value}}$$

Investor ratios

Equity ratios

An investor is interested in:

- the income earned by the company for him
- the return on his investment.

For an ordinary shareholder the relevant information will be contained in the following ratios:

Dividends	Earnings
Dividend Per Share (DPS)	Earnings Per Share (EPS)
Dividend cover	PE ratio
Dividend yield	
Total Shareholder return (TSR)	

Measure	Formula	Use
EPS	$\dfrac{\text{Profit after tax and after preference dividends}}{\text{Number of ordinary shares in issue}}$	It is the amount of profit attributable to each ordinary share.
PE ratio	$\dfrac{\text{Share price}}{\text{EPS}}$	It expresses the amount shareholders are prepared to pay for the share as a multiple of current earnings.
DPS	$\dfrac{\text{Total ordinary dividend (interim and final)}}{\text{Total number of shares issued}} \times 100$	Shows shareholders how much of the overall dividend payout they are entitled to.
Dividend Yield	$\dfrac{\text{DPS}}{\text{Market price per share at the start of the year}}$	The annual dividend per share expressed as an annual rate of return on the share price.
Dividend Cover	$\dfrac{\text{Profit available for ordinary shareholders}}{\text{Dividend for the year (interim and final)}}$	Measures how many times companies earnings could pay the dividend.
TSR	$\dfrac{\text{DPS + change in share price}}{\text{Share price at start of period}}$	Measures the returns to the investor by taking account of dividend income and capital growth.

Potential problems

ROCE

- Uses profit, not maximisation of shareholder wealth.

EPS

- Does not represent actual income.
- Uses earnings not wealth.

ROE

- Uses profits not maximisation of shareholder wealth.
- Sensitive to gearing levels.

Dividend yield

- Ignores capital growth.

Exam focus

Using financial ratios will likely be a key part of any question on:

- working capital management
- sources of finance
- business valuations
- assessing performance against objectives.

Good examples can be found in the following recent FM (previously known as F9) exams:

- June 2013 – GXG Co
- June 2014 – CSZ Co
- Sep / Dec 2015 – KQK Co

20

Business valuations and market efficiency

In this chapter

- Asset-based valuations.
- Dividend valuation model (DVM).
- Price earnings ratio method.
- Discounted cash flow basis.
- Valuation of debt and preference shares.
- The efficient market hypothesis.

Key Point

Remember valuations are subjective and a compromise between the buyer and seller.

Asset-based valuations

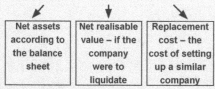

| Net assets according to the balance sheet | Net realisable value – if the company were to liquidate | Replacement cost – the cost of setting up a similar company |

Weaknesses

- These methods will usually give you a value, considerably lower than the market value of all the company's shares (the market capitalisation value).

- So it should be obvious that shareholders/the market does not value the company on the basis of the balance sheet's net asset figure. **They are not buying the company for its assets but for the income those assets can produce**.

- Difficult to incorporate/value intangible assets such as a highly skilled workforce, strong management team, competitive positioning of the company's products and goodwill. These are usually ignored, but they should account for the premium that earning-based valuations give over asset-based valuations.

Uses:

- To value companies that are going to be asset stripped or closed down.

- To set a minimum price in a takeover bid.

- To value property investment companies.

Dividend valuation model (DVM)

The value of the company/share is the present value of the expected future dividends discounted at the shareholders required rate of return.

Either:
$$P_o = \frac{d_o}{r_e} \qquad P_o = \frac{d_o(1+g)}{r_e-g}$$

Assuming:
a constant dividend or constant growth in dividends

P_o = Value of company, when

d_o = Total dividends

r_e = shareholders' required return, expressed as a decimal

g = annual growth rate

The market capitalisation is found by multiplying its current share price by the number of shares in issue.

Weakness of the DVM

- The problem of estimating a future growth rate.

- Assumes that growth will be constant in the future; this is not true of most companies.

- The model is highly sensitive to changes in its assumptions.

DVM is useful when valuing a minority stake because minorities have access to dividends, not earnings nor the company's assets.

Price-earnings ratio method

Value of company = Total earnings x P/E ratio.

Value per share = EPS x P/E ratio.

Use an adjusted P/E multiple from a similar quoted company (or industry average).

Problems

- May need make an adjustment(s) to the P/E ratio and earnings figures of the similar company to make it more suitable – give your reasons! For example:

- P/E ratios of similar listed companies are applied to the earnings of unlisted companies. However, an investment in an unlisted company can be difficult to sell (ill-liquid) so is not as desirable as an investment in a listed company. Typically, the P/E ratios are therefore reduced by 1/4 to 1/3 before being used to account for unlisted companies being less desirable.

- P/E ratios are in part based upon historical accounting information (the EPS).

Discounted cash flow basis

Key Point

Theoretically this is the best method.

The information required to calculate a company-wide NPV is:

- details of all future company cash flows
- the company discount rate, or enough information so that we can use CAPM to calculate it.

Method:

1. Identify relevant 'free' cash flows (i.e. excluding financing flows)

    - operating flows
    - revenue from sale of assets
    - tax

- synergies arising from any merger.

2 Select a suitable time horizon.

3 Calculate the PV over this horizon. This gives the value to all providers of finance, i.e. equity + debt.

4 Deduct the value of debt to leave the value of equity.

Weaknesses of the NPV method

- It relies on estimates of both cash flows and discount rates.

- What time period should we evaluate in detail and then how do you value the company's worth beyond this period i.e. the realisable value at the end of the planning period?

- The NPV method does not evaluate further options that may occur within the business.

- It assumes that the discount rate and tax rates are constant through the period.

Valuation of debt and preference shares

The dividend valuation model equations seen in chapter 15 can be re-arranged to derive market value as follows:

Preference shares MV $= \dfrac{D}{Kp}$

Irredeemable debt MV $= \dfrac{I}{Kd}$

Redeemable debt MV = PV of future interest + redemption receipts, discounted at the investors' required return.

Where
MV = Market value
PV = Present value
I = Interest
D = Dividend
Kp = Cost of preference shares
Kd = Pre tax cost of debt = investors required return

The efficient market hypothesis

Definition

An efficient market is one in which security prices fully reflect all available information, and new information is rapidly and rationally incorporated in an unbiased way into share prices.

Weak form

- Share prices reflect all known publicly available past information about companies and their shares.

- It should be impossible to predict future share price movements from historical patterns because all historical information is reflected in the current price.

- Share prices follow random walks (NOT the same as saying that share prices are irrational!)

- The next change in share price could be either upwards or downwards, with equal probability, depending on the nature of the next information made available to the market.

Semi-strong form

- Current share prices reflect not only historical share price information and other historical information about a company, but also respond immediately to other current publicly-available information about the company.

- Thus a stock market specialist who attempts to use his expertise to use the publicly available information to predict which shares will be worth buying, would have little success in out-guessing the market as the market has already assimilated that information and it is already reflected in the share price.

Chapter 20

- The evidence also tends to confirm that the semi-strong form of efficiency does exist in leading stock markets.

Strong form

- The current share price reflects all the information relevant to the company, including information that has not yet been made public – inside information!
- If the hypothesis is correct then the mere publication of the information should have no impact on the share price, consequently it should not be possible to make profits by dealing in response to inside information.
- It is unlikely that strong-form exists.

The market paradox – investors assess information which is immediately reflected in the share price. This assessment is required to ensure the market is efficient but it prevents investors from beating the market.

Herding (some investors just follow trends)

Stock market bubble (unsustainable rise in price of an investment)

Noise traders (those who follow trends rather than make professional decisions)

Loss aversion (those whose focus is to avoid a loss rather than make a gain)

Momentum effect (e.g. a trend of rising prices leads to optimism and further rising prices)

Further factors to consider when valuing shares

- Marketability and liquidity.
- Available information.
- Equilibrium prices.

KAPLAN PUBLISHING

163

Recent FM (previously known as F9) exams to cover the topics in this chapter include:

- December 2010 – Nugfer Co
- December 2010 – NN Co
- December 2011 – Close Co
- June 2012 – Corhig Co
- December 2014 – Par Co
- June 2015 – Chad Co
- Sep / Dec 2015 – Gemlo Co
- Mar / Jun 2016 – Darlga Co
- September 2016 – Ring Co (Qs 21 – 25)
- December 2016 – Coral Co (Qs 21 – 25)
- Mar / Jun 2019 – Bluebell Co

Index